Grandma's Potpourri

By Pearl Klusman

TEACH Services, Inc.
P U B L I S H I N G
www.TEACHServices.com • (800) 367-1844

World rights reserved. This book or any portion thereof may not be copied or reproduced in any form or manner whatever, except as provided by law, without the written permission of the publisher, except by a reviewer who may quote brief passages in a review.

The author assumes full responsibility for the accuracy of all facts and quotations as cited in this book. The opinions expressed in this book are the author's personal views and interpretations, and do not necessarily reflect those of the publisher.

This book is provided with the understanding that the publisher is not engaged in giving spiritual, legal, medical, or other professional advice. If authoritative advice is needed, the reader should seek the counsel of a competent professional.

Copyright © 2018 Pearl Klusman

Copyright © 2018 TEACH Services, Inc.

ISBN-13: 978-1-4796-0961-1 (Paperback)

ISBN-13: 978-1-4796-0962-8 (ePub)

Library of Congress Control Number: 2018942059

Table of Contents

Abraham Lincoln	5
A Light That Shines	7
A Little Boy	8
A Little Green Frog	9
A Loving Creator	10
A New Day	12
A New Home Awaits	13
Another Year	15
A Parched Plain	16
A Visit	17
Awake, Oh, Sleeping World	18
Awesome God	19
Birthdays	20
Blackbird	21
Burdened?	22
California	23
Congregation Prayers	24
Control the Tongue	25
Dallas	26
Dark Night	27
Darts	28
Death	29
Death Sleep	30
Devastation	31
Flickering Flame	32
Goodbye, Dear Friends	33
Haiku	34
Hail! Oh Mighty King	35
Happy Birthday	36
Happy Day	37
He Died for Me	38
Help Me Believe	39
Help Me Out	40
He Set Us Free	41
He's the Father and I'm His Child	42
I Heard the Bells A' Ringing	43
I'll Walk With the Lord	44
I'll Walk With You	45
I'm A' Going	46
Immortal Love	47
Intrusion From Yester-year	48
I Sought To Hear	49
It Is Tradition	50
I Will Praise the Lord	51
Jesus Came to Our Church	52
Jesus Our Hope	54
Kite	55
Knocking	56
Life Fades	57
Life's Rhythm	59
Little Dove	60
Little Rabbit	61
Living Water	62
Mighty God	63
Morning Visitor	64
Mother Mine	65
Mothers	66

My God Is Big Enough ... 67	The Bible 106
My Redeemer 68	The Butterfly 107
Nine/Eleven 69	The Garden Temptation 108
Ode to a Hummingbird ... 70	
Ode to a Rose 71	The Lord Is Coming 110
Oh, Wonder of Ages 72	The Lord's Message 111
Paschal Lamb 73	The Mirror 112
Passing Time 75	The Tree 113
Pebbles 76	Thou Creator 114
Pray 77	Thy Word 115
Precious Name 78	Thy Word A Light 116
Proverbs by Pearl 79	Time of Growing 117
Rain 83	'Tis Christmas 118
Reapers 84	'Tis Gone 119
Rebirth 85	Trusting God 120
Rending Sorrow 86	To Be or Not To Be 123
Revolving Earth 87	Trust 124
Shepherds Haste 88	Two Sons in The Vineyard 125
Short Verses by Pearl 89	
Silently, the Flocks of Sheep 91	Under His Wing 126
	Vanity 127
Simon of Cyrene, to his beloved sons, Alexander and Rufus 92	Wandering With a Dream 128
	Weep Tears of Joy 129
Sisters 95	When Gone This Day 130
Sleep Little Ones 96	When I'm Gone 131
Snow Mobile 97	When Life Is Gone 132
Song of the Seraphim 100	Where Can I Find Thee? . 133
Sowing Seed 101	Why Me, Lord? 134
Spring 102	With Tearful Eyes 135
Step by Step 103	Wonders of Spring 136
Take Me Home 104	You Watch Over Me 137
Tell Me Shepherds 105	

Abraham Lincoln

The cabin was made of hand hewn logs,
One room was all it had,
But the hearth was warm and hearts were, too,
When born a little lad.

Sister Sally sat on the old bear rug.
Her heart was filled with joy.
"Abraham Lincoln," Pa Thomas said,
So they named their little boy.

He learned to toil when the sun was up,
To hunt and plant and plow,
To chop the wood and ride the horse,
To feed and milk the cow.

His very first pants were buckskin.
Pa and Ma had tanned the hide.
"Buckskin is for men," the young Abe said,
And he wore those pants with pride.

With a bit of charcoal and a wooden slate,
He learned to read and write,
And he often sat by the old fireplace
To study by its flickering light.

Now Abe grew tall like a willow tree.
His legs were long and lean.
He split a thousand rails one time,
To pay for a pair of jeans.

He wrestled with the toughest men,
And threw them to the ground.
Then everyone declared that Abe
Was the strongest man around.

The children loved this tall, gaunt man,
Known for his honesty.
His funny ways and jokes he told
Are part of history.

Farmer, clerk merchant, lawyer, orator,
Captain in the Indian war,
Legislature, congressman and president,
No man ever did more.

The Northern states declared, long and loud,
"All men are created equal and free."
"Not so," cried the Southern states. "We'll secede."
And they started their own country.

Then Lincoln led his nation in a Civil War
Until that work was done.
He was shot one night in a theater bright,
And died by an assassin's gun.

A Light That Shines

A light that shines on the perfect way,
Shadows eclipse but soon pass away.
Stand fast—in darkness do not stay.
Nor to your glory yet ascribe
The height and depth of grace
God's love can thus provide.
Complete the devastation,
Soiled and shame filled heart,
Where sin did once abide,
Freed by grace, and called by God,
"You are mine."

A Little Boy

There is a little boy,
He isn't very tall,
But if he keeps on growing,
He'll get there after all.

His cheeks are red.
His hair is light.
His eyes are deep pools,
Dancing, merry, and bright.

His feet go pitter-patter
From morning until night.
He doesn't like to sleep a'tall,
As long as it is light.

He is so like his father.
He is the only one.
He is a dancing little elf,
He is my only son.

From morning until night,
His feet go pitter-patter.
Of his mother and his father,
He is so like the latter.

A Little Green Frog

A little green frog,
"Croak, croak."
Sat on the bank by the lake.
"Croak, croak."
The mud felt good
To his little webbed toes,
As he dined on exotic bugs.
"Croak, croak."
Life for him was great,
As he sang by the lake.
"Croak, croak."
And a chorus was heard,
As he was joined in his song.
"Croak, croak."
A laddie, rather late,
Strolled by the lake.
And heard the
"Croak, croak, croak."
Bending low, he
Picked up a stone to throw.
Now lady frog mournfully
Croaks all alone.
"Croak, croak."
And sorrowful to hear
Is her lonesome song.
"Croak, croak."
How sad was the lad,
For the green frog nevermore
Would sing his joyful
"Croak, croak, croak."
"Croak, croak."

A Loving Creator

A condensed version of the Bible story

All Heaven was in a joyful, expectant mood. The last five and even into the sixth day the angels had watched with mounting excitement as Father, Son, and Holy Spirit had prepared the setting for the coming event.

Every sense was to be delighted, soft rustling leaves, shimmering lakes, gems each holding their own little splash of glory, tiny delicate blossoms, bright beds of flowers, fragrant scents on every breeze, trees laden with fruit and nuts, grapes hanging in clusters, berries sparkling like jewels against the dark green of the vine, snatches of melody as birds flitted through the air or sang lustily from the branches of a nearby tree: tiny ant, gentle deer, mammoth elephant, gifts so lovingly prepared, expressions of the heart of their givers.

Angels watched in breathless wonder as new earth, fresh from the creation, was molded—not into another angel creature, but into the likeness of their God: handsome, strong, but oh, so still. God bent and with his breath gave life. Stirring, man beheld the loving face of His Creator, and their hearts were knit one to another.

God looked on waiting patiently to give again to His beloved, His joy and His delight. Man's eyelids closed in slumber soon to wake again and in waking beheld fair and dainty woman: flesh of his flesh, bone of his bone. As happy angels sang for joy, God said, "All is good." So came the Sabbath of creation.

But danger lurked there in the garden. The woman left her husband's side and wandered near the tree of knowledge where Lucifer, once the morning star, now the fallen angel, using a serpent as a medium, called to her in a voice so sweet, enticing, entreating her to eat, to be like God, knowing good and evil. Taking, Eve ran back to Adam, bid him join in her transgression. Bright robes of glory disappeared. Now naked, hid they in the garden. In fear and trembling, hid they from the God who loved them.

The seeds of sin thus planted, burst forth as Cain slew his brother, Abel. Burst forth in lies and stealing, cursing, broken hearts and broken homes, loving selves and hating brothers. So sin grew from generation to generation and quickly spread with war and strife on every hand. And sin, when it is finished, brings forth death and death passed on to all mankind.

Father, Son and Holy Spirit, still loving Their creation, desiring that none should perish, called and searched and pleaded. Taking sins from all who'd give them. Shielding, fencing in their children, clothing them in righteousness and faith and power.

Then burdened with these sins of men, with beaten back, thorn pierced brow, spit upon, nailed to the cross, in deep despair, Christ died. And in dying gained the victory that man, His beloved, might choose to live. For God is love, and love grants the right to choose.

A New Day

There's a new day.
It will pass away.
Come out and play
Before it's gone.

Hold tight each hour.
Though it may shower,
A seed will flower
To brighten another day.

You have a part:
A smile to start,
To warm some heart,
And cheer someone today.

A New Home Awaits

The place that you will soon call home
Awaits your presence there.
The pastures green, the trees in bloom,
They need your tender care.

Much calmer there, the way will be.
You've surely earned your rest.
And we, your family in the Lord,
Have truly been most blessed.

You've comforted us in sorrows;
You've shared our many tears.
You've rejoiced in all our pleasures—
So many through the years.

The work must have seemed ne'er ceasing,
As you ran from here to there.
Three churches, what a burden,
Always needing you somewhere.

Camp-outs, flea markets, and committees,
Meetings without measure,
Buying our church and helping it grow,
Memories we'll always treasure.

The paths of people touching our lives,
So many just fade away,
But the ones you've left are in our hearts.
Those prints are there to stay.

Although I'm sure you'll miss us
Once in a great while,
May remembering only bring to you,
A pleasant, happy smile.

And so we bring our blessings
To give to you today.
Goodbye, dear Pastor,
May we meet again someday.

Another Year

Another year is almost here,
With all its pain and sorrow.
What say; but nay?
We make our own tomorrow.
A word, a praise, a thoughtful deed.
A blessing to both us and others.
Pass on but good by every word;
Help uplift a brother.
The day is near when Christ appears,
Our woes be gone forever.
"Peace on earth," the angels sang,
On that night so long ago.
Peace will come as hearts relate
To our God above us.

A Parched Plain

Wild, clashing thunder,
Echoing across a parched plain,
Gives but promise of life giving rain.
Splatter,
But a few drops fall,
The earth athirst remains.
Send Thy Spirit, Lord.
Revive us,
Lest we perish like the grain.

A Visit

I went to visit tonight,
A friend to me so dear.
I thought that I would bring
To her a little cheer.
Upon the door I lightly knocked.
"Come in, come in,
Come in, my dear."
A friendly welcome, warm and kind
Upon poor me was lavished.
The gift I sought to give was rags,
Pure gold on me was showered.
We sang of the Savior's love.
The Spirit filled the hour.
Go to cheer this friend? Not I.
I'll go again—my own heart
To be lifted high.

Awake, Oh, Sleeping World

Awake, oh, sleeping world, awake.
Awake, rejoice and sing.
With joyful hearts and light, arise.
Your King decendeth through the skies.

Awake, oh, sleeping world, awake.
Cast off thy heavy weight of sin.
Welcome Him with loving heart.
His promise is, "I'll come again."

No need to ask, "Where is He?"
For that event all eyes will see
As righteous meet Him in the sky.
"Oh, rocks hide me," the wicked cry.

No, He'll not come at will of men,
But to take His loved ones home with Him.
Awake, oh, sleeping world, awake and sing.
Prepare to meet your Heavenly King.

Awesome God

My God is so awesome;
Righteous and loving is He.
Oh, how I love Him, my wonderful God.
He's quick to forgive when I am bad.
When I obey, He rejoices—is glad.
Oh, how I love Him, my Heavenly King.
Patient and kind;
Wants me to mind,
And rewards all my efforts with blessings divine.
Oh, how I love Him, this dear Lord of mine.
If we desire not to grieve Him,
We need only look.
He has written it down in His Holy Book.

Birthdays

Birthdays count the years you add
To this life's earthly stay.
And if by chance you're running well
When birthdays come your way,
You can pat yourself upon your back,
"Well done! Well done!" can say.
So, we're wishing you,
With all our hearts,
A grand and happy day.

Blackbird

A blackbird sat in a tree.
He sang a song;
He sang it for me.
I sat up in bed.
I hear blackbird sing.
"It is spring. It is spring."
I put on my robe, ran to the door.
I ran as fast as my feet would go.
"Where are you blackbird?"

I looked in the tree.
Blackbird is looking right down at me.
Then he sang it again.
"It is spring. It is spring."
He looked once again
Then flew up in the sky.
How that blackbird could fly.
"Bye-bye, blackbird. Blackbird, bye-bye."

Burdened?

Do at times you feel o'er burdened?
Do you feel a cross you bear?
Do you feel nobody knows it?
Do you feel nobody cares?
Jesus sends the answer.
It's not the one you thought.
"Take up your cross and carry it.
Do not let it drop.
I know it will grow heavy,
But you must struggle on.
I cannot take it from you
If you want a victory won.
But I can walk beside you
And lend a helping hand.
We'll walk along together
Until we reach the promised land."

California

On desert bare, but cacti grow,
There sits owlet nesting in the thorn.
Cut, the sand, with dirt bike trails,
Where once coyote howled.

In the distance, Sierra's peak,
White clad with winter still adorned.
Spring's warm call wakens rushing streams,
That to the valley flow, and on they go,
To reach Pacific shore.

Where beachers come in droves to vie
For waves, or sand, or shell long cleaned,
Of some small denizen of the deep.
'Til all remains a broken shell—
Treasure in some laddie's pail, desires to keep.

Mounts, desert, sea, and stream,
And asphalt trails, so many lanes,
Jungles—tall towers instead of trees
Where humans live and prowl.
Cities large and towns quite small,
California has them all.

Forlorn—nay not so.
For nature full-adorned in finery all her own,
Beckons, calls forth to come and see,
That which desert alone can show.

Congregation Prayers

Mighty God, Thy love has drawn us;
But we have sinned against Thee.
Be gracious unto us and wash away our guilt.
Give us pure hearts.
Give us the Holy Spirit to direct our paths,
And hold back the evil one.

We thank Thee for the care Thou does give daily;
The wisdom that comes alone from Thee;
The rain in season and the sunshine; for food and shelter;
For all these we thank Thee.

With loving trust, we bring to Thee our ill, our hurting,
Our financial and our physical needs;
Our family member that our heart yearns to see saved;
Church members that have fallen away,
We place them in Your hands. Thy will be done.
In the blessed name of Jesus, we pray.

Control the Tongue

Many problems between adults and youth are found in the attitude adults use when responding to behavior. Adults want immediate obedience, and a command seems the quickest way to get it. It is often spoken in irritation or even anger. A command can be demeaning, embarrassing, or deflating—showing a lack of trust. The tone of voice, or body language, can have the same effect. These in turn can trigger a defiant defense.

The Bible has much to say about the tongue. It's deceitful, defiles the body, is a world of iniquity, poison as an asp.

<u>Our defense against this tongue</u>
"A good shepherd lays down his life for the sheep."
Gently leads.
"Out of the abundance of the heart the mouth speaks."
"I can do all things through Christ."
"With lovingkindness will draw all men."
"Honor one another."

<u>With these admonitions before us, our response to our family should be Christ-like.</u>
Our speech should be
Approved of God.
Honor one another.
Respectful
Uplifting.
Merciful.

The world was created by the word—there is great power in the word, for good or for evil.

Dallas

I met a man whose heart was love.
In all he did, he showed it—
A cheery smile, a helping hand,
Or just a Dunkin' Donut®.

He passed no man without a "Hi,"
No child without he hugged it.
With generous hand he spread his wealth;
With humble heart, he shared it.

His time, the Lord's, he freely gave
In service for another.
To save a soul his delight—
He called all men his brother.

His earthly aim—to walk with God.
He served Him day and night.
The gift of love God gave to him.
He shared with pure delight.

Dark Night

Oh, Son of God, Holy Light,
My path is dark as darkest night.
The hidden trail, I cannot see.
I'm lost in deep despair.
Oh, Light of God, guide Thou me.

Shine through the clouds:
My path do clearly show.
You know the way that I should go.
To will and do are gifts from You.
The path You choose, I would pursue.

Oh, Star of Glory, oh, Holy Light,
Guide this weary traveler,
Through the dark, dark night.
There is a trail I cannot see.
I wish, my God, to follow Thee.

Darts

I would that from my lips spill forth
Words in joy, to lift a wounded soul;
Or spring forth, a well of wisdom that
Confused minds might behold,
And rest.
Should I utter words of comfort,
Peace would come to some,
Or softly speak
To soothe a savage, troubled breast.
Cry aloud! Oh, soul!
For none of these escape thy lips,
But burst some word to thrust,
To hurt.
And darts, poison tipped,
Where e'er I tread, hast found a goal,
And wounded lie along the path.
Oh! Weep, my soul.

Death

'Ere one is born death lingers near,
Craving yet another soul,
And all along life's thorny road,
Oft it reaches out, again withholds.
Life ebbs and flows.

Babes, youth, or tottering age,
It matters not, death would welcome
Close within earth's bosom.
There to hold, in sleep forevermore.
But, nay not so.

"A little while," thus saith the Lord.
So, dear one, sleep on
'Til trumpet calls you
From your earthly grave,
And shrouds of darkness thus unfold.

Then springing forth
Like flower from a seed,
We shall behold our Savior's face.
Death shall flee to be no more.

Death Sleep

I stared death full in the face today
And felt no fear.
I did not know that it would be that way.
For oft I thought of a dark and lonely trail
With no end near,
That led on and on to an endless vale,
Haunted by the cries of lost souls
Wondering there.
And what I saw—t'was not so.
But rest, sweet rest, held in close embrace
In the bosom of the earth,
Waiting the Savior's call to a new morn.
So content am I to sleep on.

In the garden of my mind,
A memory is planted there,
And I shall often open the door
And of its fragrance share.
We had you such a little while,
Tho' a woman grown, still you seemed so young,
But now you're gone.
'Til morning come, dear one, sleep on.

Devastation

Complete the devastation,
Where sin did once abide.
Soiled and shame-filled heart,
Freed by grace,
Such a one was I.
Yet, called by God, "You are Mine."
Mercy showed a better way.
Now, near my God I wish to stay.

Flickering Flame

In each heart, there burns a flicker of a flame.
Will you tend it? Help it grow?
Or smother it by life's wiles?
And cry at life's end, "I did not know."

Goodbye, Dear Friends

They are about to leave us,
Our friends who are most dear.
We will let them go.
We would not hold them here.

Sabbath we will come to church.
We'll look all around—
No Jennifer, no Linda,
And no Dan will be found.

We are going to miss them
As they go their way.
But when the Master calls them,
Who will say Him nay?

For He it is that charts the course.
He that sets the sails.
He sees you through the calm
And keeps in blustery gales.

And when you reach the port
Where now you are a going,
What He has for you to do,
There is no way of knowing.

But adventure there awaits you,
When you serve the Lord.
For in service for your Master,
You never will get bored.

Although I'm sure you'll miss us,
Once in a great while,
May remembering only bring to you,
A pleasant, happy smile.
And so we bring our blessing here,
To give to you today.
Goodbye, goodbye, dear friends.
Haste, haste you on your way.

Haiku

Pipe red plums,
Soaring, shimmering heat,
Jars on a shelf.

Dawn in the north,
Shimmering, dancing,
Crane enticing.

Hiding places.
Nap of rug.
Fleas and roaches.

Willows, limber, swaying,
Sandy beach,
Half-buried boat.

Tender breeze,
Open window,
Old lady sleeping.

Laden branches, rotting fruit,
Steaming jars,
Little boy dancing.

Clear water,
Streaks of darting color,
A second sky.

Snow-capped peaks,
Dawn pink,
A rooster crows.

Hail! Oh Mighty King

Hail! Oh Mighty King.
Before Thee we humbly bow.
Hail! Oh King of Kings and universe.
Bless us now. Bless us now.
How can human lips proclaim,
Or call Thee Lord of Lords?
For evil sits upon our brow.
Oh! Wash us clean. Wash us clean.
We would with humble hearts adore Thee.
Great and mighty is Thy power.
Clothe us in Thy righteousness,
This very hour. This very hour.
Hail! Oh Mighty King.
The Living Word
Hail! Thee whom we adore,
The Morning Star.
To Thee our praise and honor bring.
To Thee our anthems raise.
Oh Son of God. Oh Son of God.

Happy Birthday

The year has gone so quickly.
It seems no time at all.
Ahead of you, the future still
Is yours to shape and call.
And as you make sour plans, my dear,
Remember God's ten rules.
Keeping God's commandments
Are the best of building tools.

Happy Day

Each day is a happy day,
When walked beside our Lord.
Each day is a happy day,
Lived in obedience to His Word.

Sheltered by His wings are we;
Fed by His loving hand;
Guided through our daily chores,
A happy Christian band.

Trials will come and heartache, too.
Long will seem the road.
Take up your cross and follow on.
He'll lift the heavy load.

Tears that now doth flood the eyes,
Will turn to shouts of joy,
When ten thousand angels do appear,
And Christ in all His glory.

Once He came as a tiny babe.
In humble form was He.
He bore our hurt, our sin, our curse.
He died nailed to a tree.

Now He reigns, a King of Kings.
A Lord of Lords is He.
He's coming back for those He loves.
He loves both you and me.

He Died for Me

The hosts of heaven hid their faces,
Tears down their cheeks did roll.
How could it be? How could it be
That they would treat dear Jesus so?
The Prince of Heaven, nailed for all to see.
How could it be and yet was so.
Excruciating pain, nailed to a tree.

Blood streamed from every slash severe.
Cruel soldiers lashed and flogged with zeal.
Muscles strained with every blow,
That nailed Him there upon the tree
How could it be and yet t'was so.
The Prince of Heaven, nailed for all to see.

I do not know. I cannot know.
How suffering, Christ would die for me!
He came, my ransom thus to pay.
Thus, bearing my sin, set me free.
For me, for me, how could it be?
Beaten, blow on blow,
And I the one who was let go.
My life, dear Lord, I give to Thee.

He came to teach me a better way.
He came my ransom thus to pay,
And I the one who was let go.
My life, dear Lord, I give to Thee,
Weak and sinful though I be,
May Thy spirit give me power,
To live for Thee each day, each hour.

Help Me Believe

Jesus! Jesus!
Help Thou my unbelief.
Jesus! Jesus!
My soul doeth truly weep.
Send Thy Spirit as Thou dids't so long ago.
Jesus! Jesus!
Send Thy Spirit that my heart may truly know.
That I can go when Thou does't come
To live with Thee in Heaven.

Jesus! Jesus!
Give me rest.
Take from me my doubting breast.
Jests! Jesus! I long to know
That Thou accepts this wayward soul.
Send Thy Spirit, full of grace,
To fill this heart, each empty space,
And flood from there
Throughout this soul.

Thou has't said to call on Thee:
In faith, I call; in faith, believe;
And, by Thy Grace, in faith, receive.
Thank Thee, Jesus. Thank Thee.
Praise and glory fill my frame.
Pour forth now in living streams.
Jesus! Jesus!
May I not come to Thy Heavenly gates alone.
Holy Spirit, freely given,
Shared with others, leads to Heaven.

Help Me Out

Thou Lord, knowest the recesses of the heart.
Nothing is hid there from Thee.
Thou beholdest the sadness and sorrow there,
Sheltered where none else can see.

The body stands guard with a shield of strife,
Counting all but a deadly foe.
Striking with anger, malice, and doubt,
Any who might see the woe.

For a sinful, lost soul cowers deeply in fear,
Wanting all else to exclude.
Oh, love of God! Help me out! Help me out!
I'm lost in this dreadful, dark mood.

May my sword of defense be one of Your love,
And my shield, complete trust in Thee.
The helmet I wear, do away with all doubt,
For Thou are my life and sure victory.

He Set Us Free

Praise our God, He set us free.
Long years prophesied Isaiah, "He will come, Emanuel."
The wise men from the East came seeking,
Seeking they the Prince of Peace.
Following they the guiding star,
Leading always to the west.
Long they walked both dark and dawn,
Following the light that led them on.
Until at last in a manger lay,
One small babe in fresh new hay.
Of myrrh and frankincense,
They brought the best.
What gift have we that we can bring?
What gift have we fit for a King?
No myrrh or frankincense will do.
The gift He asks, dear friend, is you.
Your heart, your life will serve quite well.
Then He will always with you dwell.
He asks no more; will take no less.
And in its place your life He'll bless.
Christmas is a happy day, a merry day,
And all because of one small babe who lay,
Swaddled in a manger full of fresh new hay.
Lord of Lords and King of Kings was He,
But left His home and former majesty.
He came to earth—a gift for you and me.

He's the Father and I'm His Child

He is the Father, and I'm His child.
He'll still the waves when the ocean's wild.
He'll light the pathway when dark prevails.
He'll hold my hand when doubt assails.
      For He's the Father,
        and I'm His child.

He can multiply my daily bread
And take away the fear and dread.
He can give me wisdom to walk each day—
His Word a light to lead the way.
      For He's the Father,
        and I'm His child.

His promise is He will provide;
I need only walk close at His side.
I need no sun or moon for light.
For where He is there is no night.
      For He's the Father,
        and I'm His child.

He is my Friend, my daily Guide.
When I stumble, He'll never chide.
Away old world! Off and away!
I see the dawn of a bright new day.
      For He's the Father,
        and I'm His child.

I Heard the Bells A' Ringing

I heard the bells a' ringing,
Carols filled the air.
Shining lights in colors bright,
Outshone the twinkling stars of night.
Though weather wet and dreary,
There was joy everywhere.
Life seemed wrapped in pleasure;
Having fun, the gift to treasure.
A time to revel and to play,
So people went their happy way.
Oh, you who love your Savior;
Shout, "Hosanna, Jesus is our King."
For the Gift that came to Bethlehem
To show us a better way,
That great Gift awaits us still.
Welcome Him this Christmas Day.

I'll Walk With the Lord

I will walk, walk, walk with the Lord.
I will talk, talk, talk with the Lord.
On my face will appear not a frown.
If I fall in a pit, it won't get me down.
No fear will I show, as onward I go,
As I walk, walk, walk with the Lord.
My God is big enough to handle the trials.
My God is big enough to handle the woes,
And anything else old Satan throws.
Why should I tremble with fears?
Why bathe my face in endless tears?
No arrow can pierce, no plague can come near,
His shadow a shelter, His word a shield.
So I'll walk, walk, walk with the Lord.
Never falter or fear, 'til He takes me home.

I'll Walk With You

"I'll walk with you," the Savior said.
"Don't halt nor fear the thorn.
Though rough the path and long it seems,
You need not walk alone."

"With many a weary wanderer I've walked,
Oft' this treacherous way.
Just travel with me though it seems long,
We'll reach a bright new day."

"When discouraged and lonely reach out.
To my hand, hang on,
When your feet falter, and you scarce can stand.
Again I say, 'Hang on, hang on.'"

"I know the hurt from shattered dreams,
When down your cheek the tears do flow.
And each deep despair, how dark it seems.
I weep, too, the pain I know."

'There is a place at the end of the trail
With pleasures you never did dream.
The pain and the heartache soon will be gone,
And you'll drink from the life-giving stream."

"We'll travel together life's dusty road.
You never need to walk it alone.
Feint not at the mountains, nor dark ravines.
Hang on! We're almost home."

I'm A' Going

I'm a' going; I'm a' going;
I'm a' going to the Promised Land,
For Jesus will take me there.
He'll be coming; He'll be coming;
He'll be coming with His angels bright.
With the clouds on high, I'll rise.
For I'm a' going to the Promised Land
With Jesus.

Immortal Love

Glory to the Father,
Whose heart for us does yearn;
So He sent to us down here below,
His one and only Son.

His love has kindled in our heart,
A light to brightly burn;
A light to lead us through the dark,
And guide us safely home.

A home where He is waiting,
With mansions bright and fair;
A heart that's full of yearning,
For us to join Him there.

Bring praise, honor, and glory,
To the Father on His throne;
Immortal love forever,
In His heart is born.

In reverence before Him bow;
In praise our voices ring.
He is Creator, Mighty God,
Our Master and our King.

Intrusion From Yester-year

What's that sound so softly drifting?
'Tis foreign to the ear.
The scene no such invites.
From whence it cometh? Do you hear?
For whose ear doth it soundeth?
No one turns to acknowledge nor to see.
No one seems to hear nor wonder—only me.
The tall man rests with lifted foot
Resting on a rustic beam,
Full engrossed in scene before him spread,
As children play on neighbor's lawn.
Their laughter quite erases the sound.
Or is there such?
I wonder with cocked ear.
Or just a fleeting memory of the past,
Imposing on a present time and place,
So softly drifting on some inner ear.
Some memory long thought 'twas erased
Would haunt today and find a place.
But would I dare to search the sound?
What paths might ope' in reverie?
Would such I dare to trod?
Depart, oh softly drifting sound.
I do not wish to follow thee.
There are dark recesses of the past;
Gates long barred: I would intrude not there.
So again I say, "Oh sound, depart, be gone.
Lead me not along that way."

I Sought To Hear

I sought to hear
The Word of God,
With tears and supplication.

I heard it not,
Though oft I sought,
And wept in agitation.

"Thy will be done,"
At last I cried,
And God was there
Right by my side.

It Is Tradition

Sleigh bells ringing in the night,
Their song of "Ding-Ding-Dong" so bright.
Though long the sleigh departed, gone,
The song of bells just lingers on.
It is tradition.

Carolers sing in shopping malls,
Their rondo-lay of "Deck the Halls"
While beg the poor upon the street,
"Give us food that we may eat."
It is tradition.

In frantic haste the buyers stream,
To buy the things on TV seen,
And feel aggrieved when it's not found.
They hustle, bustle all around.
It is tradition.

And through windows, trees aglow,
Give promise of bright gifts below.
Anticipation grows by leap and bound,
As do wishes for snow upon the ground.
It is tradition.

The masses come to church to pray,
Not seen there any other day.
They seek some blessing from on high.
In hushed, still voice, the pious cry,
"It is tradition."

Love endowed our Christmas so,
By a babe born long ago.
Now, Our Lord, King on high,
We worship You there in the sky.
It is tradition.

I Will Praise the Lord

I will praise the Lord
        morning and evening.
I will praise the Lord
        midnight and noon.
I will praise Him when
        dark clouds o'er shadow
            And all seems covered with gloom.

I will praise the Lord
        with my voice raised in singing.
I will praise the Lord

        in the quiet hour of prayer.
I will praise Him,
        the God of creation.
            May His glory be spread everywhere.

Jesus Came to Our Church

Jesus came to our church.
'Twas two weeks ago today.
The thought within His heart was,
"Who will show the way?"

"There are children I would have,
That I would call my own.
But who will welcome them to heart?
Who will lead them home?"

He would not have them hurt,
As we hurt Him, I fear,
And so He came to our church,
Blue jeans He did wear.

Did you miss the chance to see Him?
Or turn your head and stare?
What e'er the case, I greatly fear,
He found no welcome there.

"Oh! Please depart and that right soon."
The deacon did implore.
"Our congregation soon will come,
And find standing at our door."

"Be on your way," again he said.
And hustled Him away.
Jesus sadly left our church.
Just two weeks ago today.

"I'm sorry, Lord. I did not know,
'Twas you a standing there.
Would have fallen at your feet,
Shown you every care."

"I did not recognize you Lord."
"No excuse," the Scriptures say.
"You should treat others just like Me.
You will be judged that way."

Will Jesus come a' calling
On our church again?
Will He once more alone
In our churchyard stand?

We must greet each stranger
With loving heart each day.
Then Jesus may return to our church
Two weeks from today.

Jesus Our Hope

Jesus is like the warm sun after the rains and windy storms, like a safe harbor when ocean waves do roar. When our life hits bottom and all hope is gone, He will not forsake us: He will keep us from all harm. In warning, calling, He shows us the heavenly way to rise up in victory. Have hope again today.

Kite

I saw a kite by strong winds tossed,
Leap across the sky.
Mortals, too, are buffeted,
But strong held, do safely fly
Until, in anguish to be loose,
They break the safety tie,
Then by some wayward wind are tossed
To earth to break and die.

Knocking

It's hard to remember the empty days,
The empty hours,
The empty house.
Emptiness that penetrates the soul with a sense of aloneness.
No one there.
No one to share.
No one to care.
But I only need open the door.
For Jesus long had been knocking,
And I had not heard.
Heard not a word.
Deaf to the knock of the Lord:
But in patience He stood and knocked at my door.
He would not intrude:
But, knowing my need He stood,
Knocking,
And waiting,
And calling.
Softly calling, so as not to alarm.
But rather, that the voice of love might strike some inner cord,
He, waiting, stood.
Gradually the awareness of not being alone,
Awareness of love.
I fled to the door.

Life Fades

Life just fades away into the past,
From where it first began.
A short recall, then memories wane,
With passing time, are gone.
And yet a face, a voice,
A color, or a scene,
Familiar seem.

The future, too, once filled with dreams,
Has passed and lies not so much ahead,
But fades away into an emptiness.
The future but a dream of youth,
In which we no longer share.
'Tis but the way things are.

Time marches on in tiny steps,
Or tedious strides too long.
For those who reach the stage,
Where life is ebb instead of flow,
And yester-year a memory,
Faded like some half-remembered dream,
Haunts yet a while, then too will go.

A weary body, mind, and soul,
Seek to leave life's turbulent flow,
And in some quiet nook rest awhile.
Memories mock the aged frame,
They've had their day. They've passed,
So let them go.

And death, a reward,
Hard earned by some,
Leaves torment of the mind,
And pain wracked body far behind.
So, if in passing a sigh escapes my lips,

Consider this.
There's naught to hold me here.
I would seek release, be done.

Mayhaps some wonder waits me yet,
On the other side of death's door.
In this alone lies hope. Oh! let me go.
Nor hold me here. I would pass on.

Life's Rhythm

The bird, black against the cloud,
As though in some joyful flight,
Dipped and rose and dipped again,
'Til fading in the distance, vanished out of sight.
The rhythm of the world held sway.
The clouds to some slower tune did dance,
Adding just an accent to the tempo of the bird
As he onward winged his way.
There is a rhythm in the twinkling of a star,
In the passage of the sun and moon,
As on its axis, this old world turns and spins.
It tips and sways in harmonic beat,
Bringing forth boisterous winter winds.
Bright blossoms of spring to the rhythm play.
Scorching heat of summer lends cadence to the band.
Through autumn flows the rhythm,
As falling leaves their tempo show.
Again the bird is there, closer now.
It beats a swift tattoo, then,
Folding wing, glides to the tree,
Where, perched upon the topmost bough,
To the silent rhythm of the world,
He adds a wondrous note, God given.
For this, his moment to fulfill a part,
In the song of life as it moves and sways,
Spins and turns. Soft, undulating rhythm, which
Can burst into a stormy clashing crescendo
Like beating waves awash upon the shore.
The life of man is but a part of the great flow,
The tempo, tune, and song are of God.

Little Dove

Were you watching, little dove,
In the stable, up above?
Did you watch as Joseph lay,
In a manger, fresh new hay?
Was your heart a' beating wild,
As mother Mary held the child?

Were you watching, little dove,
In the stable, up above?
Did you behold a star so bright,
As glorious angels lit the night?
Did you, the message hear on high,
As angels sang there in the sky?

Were you watching, little dove,
In the stable, up above?
Did you hear the shepherds say,
"Where is he 'twas born this day?"
Did you see them kneel before Him?
Did you see them there adore Him?

Were you watching, little dove,
As you roosted, up above?
Were you there with cow and sheep,
Did you waken from your sleep?
Were you first to welcome Him,
On that Christmas morning?

Little Rabbit

Little Briar Rabbit
Burrowed in your den,
Do you know the sun is up?
Come out and play again.
We'll scurry through the grasses,
Nibble clover here and there,
Play hide-and-seek and then,
Hurry back to mother
In her cozy den.

Living Water

Water, water, give me water,
For a parched and weary traveler,
For a tired and weary soul.
From the well that's never dry,
Give me water lest I perish,
In earth's bosom ever more to lie.
When the Lord spoke
To the woman at the well,
Never did she think,
That He would give her water,
Water from the living well to drink.

Mighty God

Mighty God, who between the cherubim does dwell,
Such love and mercy on us You do bestow,
On us who struggle here below.
A thousand ways to us You cry.
You gave us laws to keep us safe,
That we might live and never die.
Mighty God, Thy love has drawn us,
Though we have sinned against Thee.
Thy grace has washed away our guilt,
From sin has set us free.
Come soon and take us home.
Our hearts so long to be with Thee.

Morning Visitor

A cat came slinking through the grass,
So silent in the dawn.
Then stood watching, poised for flight,
As I raked the lawn.
Less cautious now, she closer moved,
So graceful in her walk.
And stopping out of reach, she stood,
Listening to me talk.
With eyes upon my face, she gazed,
Uncertain of the human 'neath the trees.
Silent then she sat and washed her face,
Accepting me.

Mother Mine

God bless you dear Mother,
As we consider on this day,
The path of life through which we
                stumbled,
As you tried to show the way.
From earliest youth, each hurt,
                with care, by you was tended.
How sweet to remember:
With a kiss, they all were mended.
In sickness, the darkness of the night
Held for us no fear,
For you, dear loving Mother,
Were always standing near.
With joy, we gathered close around
As stories of the past you did unfold.
Jewels each one, treasures hung,
On threads of purest gold.
Oh, Mother dear, the years how fleeting.
How swift they passed on by.
And when our Savior comes in glory,
Together may we meet Him in the sky.

Mothers

Mothers dear have a reputation,
Always caring,
Always loving.
There in every need.
Patient too, and kind,
Forgiving quite a lot.
Helpful when things don't go well,
And hugs that mend a broken heart.
Mothers have a reputation,
'Tis love—love that bears the cost.

My God Is Big Enough

My God is big enough
>To take care of His creation.

My God is wise enough
>To handle the problems of the nations.

My God is patient enough
>To give us room to grow.

My God is forgiving enough
>That our past need not o'erwhelm us.

My God is merciful enough
>We can have hope.

My God is loving enough
>To envelope the most unlovely.

My God is peaceful enough
>To calm the most troubled heart.

My God is joyful enough
>To bring gladness to the most oppressed.

My God is gracious enough
>To be a friend to the most needy.

My God is faithful enough
>That we need never doubt.

My God is just enough
>To destroy evil and save the righteous.

My God is generous enough
>No good thing will He withhold from them that walk uprightly.

My Redeemer

You are my Redeemer, my very life.
You decree victory over every trial for me.
My own heart is deceitful and not to be trusted;
My actions do not bring me victory.
But You give me strength to overcome,
To trample under foot every shameful temptation.
My love for You is without measure;
My desire, to glorify Your name in all I do.

The sins of my past o'erwhelm me;
The remembrance of them humbles me;
My heart faints for shame of them.
I chose as my companions those who were not wise.
I followed where they led
And was happy to join in their transgressions.
My disgrace is before me all day long.
And night is filled with pain of remembering.

Oh, that my feet had sought your path,
That my ears had been open to Your calling.
In Your compassion, You did not reject me.
In Your mercy, You paid for my transgressions.
In Your love you wrapped me in Your arms of grace
And cast the record of my filthy life into the depth of the sea.
It cannot be used to condemn me for You have decreed it so.
I am Your child, purchased at great cost,
Though unworthy I be.

Nine/Eleven

The sky is falling! The sky is falling!
Run and tell the King.
Thinketh thou He knoweth not?
Thinketh thou He cannot see?
From the falling towers people ran.
Most did not escape.
Where was the King?
Why this thing did He allow?
Did He hide Himself?
Did He not care?
As He witnessed all the sorrow there,
As He heard the cries, beheld the tears,
And saw death itself in full terror reign?
Why, Lord? Why, my God,
Did You allow such pain?
As the towers of New York came tumbling down,
Were You there? Did You care?

There were those who at work did not arrive
On that day of days.
Some little thing held them back.
Was it You, Lord?
In Your tender care,
Did You see in them some reason for delay?
Were You there on that dreadful day?

September eleven, year two thousand one, across the
nation shock waves sprung.
Eyes glued to the screen as played the scene,
And as the picture in all its horror burst,
Twin towers from the sky was thrust.
A nations pride was laid in dust.
120 stories high, a landmark in Manhattan sky.
Towers of financial strength,
Symbols of the geniuses of man to thus erect.
Shattered, gone. But memories remain.

Ode to a Hummingbird

With a whir, you entered my garden retreat.
Your tiny wings so fast they did beat,
With a whir, you hung there in the sky,
Invisible the wings to the human eye.
Such vibrant color your tiny chest displayed.
As with another whir, you took yourself away.
Did you sate yourself with nectar
From my hanging pot?
Or seek instead some bounty
Hidden in a flower's heart?
Whichever way you choose to feed,
I marvel at your wondrous speed.
And as I watched you thus today,
A marvelous blessing came my way.

Ode to a Rose

Oh rose, so beautiful, so fair,
Scenting up the evening air.
Your sweet aroma pervades the night,
And lingers on in morning light.
Your petals, soft as velvet there,
A rainbow of colors gives you flair.
And at the heart of each dear blossom,
You hide the essence of perfume.
With rainbow colors you adorn,
But also wear the hurtful thorn.
Now can it be that one so lovely, sweet.
Such pain and anguish also mete?

Oh, Wonder of Ages

Oh, wonder of ages,
Such honor to bestow,
On a wayward planet,
On a lost and sin-filled world:
Such love as only God could show.
A God Who with one thought could abolish all,
In pity would provide us grace.
No human yet can count the cost.
Of all the sins God did erase.

Paschal Lamb

The bright, full moon lit the night sky, and the people were happy for winter was gone. There would be a celebration to thank their goddess of spring, Easter, for the grass and flowers, for baby bunnies, for lambs romping in the meadows, and for all the new life around them. They colored their eggs and wore their prettiest clothes. They had wild parties and praised the goddess, who was only an idol in their heart and could neither see, nor hear. The people never even knew that God in Heaven had created the world and all the lovely things in it.

To the Israelites it was a time of celebration, too. As they looked at the big, full moon, they knew the Passover time was near. Many aunts, uncles, and cousins came to celebrate the Passover in Jerusalem, the city where the beautiful temple stood. It was a fun time especially for the children.

Fathers went to the flocks of sheep in the fields, and there they very carefully examined the lambs. The one they chose must have no cuts nor bruises. Its legs must be strong and straight, and its eyes, bright and clear. The one they chose must be the very healthiest, prettiest, liveliest lamb of the whole flock. It was to be a very special lamb. It was to be the Paschal Lamb.

The chosen lamb was brought home and given to the children to care for. The children must feed it, and water it, and keep it safe. They got to pet it, and play with it, and bathe it, even sleep with it. No wonder they had so much fun—until the day of the Passover dinner! How they cried when daddy killed the little lamb they had grown to love.

But let me tell you about the Paschal lamb. Remember the story of the Israelites? They were slaves in Egypt. God sent Moses to bring them to Jerusalem, but Pharaoh wouldn't let them go. Not even when Moses told Pharaoh that it was God who told him to let them go. Finally, God told the Israelites to kill a little lamb and put the blood on their doors. That night God sent the death angel to Egypt to make Pharaoh let His people go. The Israelites were safe behind the doors that had the blood of the little lamb for the death angel passed right over them without hurting any one of them.

We no longer need to kill the little lambs to remember a long-ago Passover for Jesus is our Paschal Lamb. He died to save us so we could live with Him forever and ever. When the full moon lights the night sky, and flowers bloom, when bunnies and lambs eat the fresh green grass in the meadow, we remember that long-ago Easter morning Jesus' friends went to His tomb and the angels told them, "He is not here. He is risen."

Passing Time

Know you not that in passing,
You add but wrinkles to the old,
And slow the step, and dim the eye?
While youth cry out, "Oh, hurry on!"
But, "Slow your pace," I cry,
"Lest I am gone."

Pebbles

I looked into a jar today,
All filled with pebbles bright.
Picked along the path of life,
Buffeted and tossed till smooth they laid,
And I, with pleasure, picked them up,
And carried them away.
I placed them in a little jar,
To look at every day.

Pray

Kneel down to pray to God in Heaven?
I don't know what to say.
I've asked for blessings all day through,
I can think now of no blessing new.
Did I forget to thank Him? No.
For help? That too, I asked.
Forgiveness? It was on my list.
I know!
"Dear Jesus, I love you."

Precious Name

The precious name of Jesus,
A gift so rich, so rare.
"Call on Me," is what He said.
"In My Name, say your prayer.
To the Father in My Name do come,
He and I still work as one.
Before the world was e'er created,
We were Spirit, Father, Son."

Together We the sorrow saw
As sin just grew and grew.
We saw its ugly tentacles enwrap,
And how engulfed were you.
Together wept We as a plan was laid.
The twining weed I must destroy,
For sinning souls, a ransom paid.
Restore again the Eden joy.

And so I came and bore the pain.
My blood destroyed thus the weed.
He who would call upon My Name,
From sin and death would be freed.
So boldly use the name of "Jesus."
When to God you pray,
Your sins will all forgiven be.
There is no other way.

Proverbs by Pearl

Parents' influence may be for evil or for good,
but the ultimate results rest on our own shoulders.

Perfect parents brought forth "Cain," but evil Nazareth "Christ."

A weak man thinketh not to travel the rough way: He putteth forth lithe cffort to attain a goal.

It's easier to find excuses than accept fault in one's self.
To save face exceeds friendship.

Misplaced loyalty is destructive to self-respect.
Choose wisely he who would be your role model.

High goals call forth super strength.

Power, riches, and beauty are heavy loads to carry through to the Kingdom.

With no destination, there is no heart to begin.

It's easier to lighten someone else's burden than to lighten your own.

Only a fool follows in the footsteps of another, when he can plainly see they lead to unstable ground.

An arrow rises no higher than the bow is aimed,
And a man no higher than his dream.

Hurting humans will do themselves harm,
and in the process will damage the people around them.

Often we take attention away from our personal issues by focusing our attention on others, making valueless judgments and character demeaning remarks.

When temptation catch your eye—flee. Don't stand and drool. Your own lust will betray you.

Satan can only tempt. Responsibility for action lies at your door.

Strong is the man who resists his own desires to evil.

With God's gifts of courage and strength, ordinary men accomplish amazing feats.

Scars, by words inflicted, are hard to erase.

We are being created daily. Resist not God's molding.

The past be gone as though it ne'er had been. Leave it gone. Enough the problems of today.

Ego is selfish, excusing self. Love is kind, excusing others.

Age wrinkles the face. Loss of enthusiasm wrinkles the soul.

Without a mental image of what we desire
only apathy pervades our soul.

With no mental picture of a want, there is no inclination to achieve.

A skinned knee receives attention; a hurting heart God's care.

Wisdom is slow and patient.
He who runs ahead of it stumbles and falls to his disgrace.

Treasure pain. It is a sign that you're living.
Experience it. It will ebb with healing.

Perspective = Seeing things from a different angle.
Try to visualize God's perspective.

Does having God mean happy ever after? No. Severe loss disrupts faith,
but God is the same yesterday, today, and forever.

Life is like crossing a river at flood stage.
It's easier to reach the other side without excess baggage.

A lazy man loves his leisure, but leisure produces no bread.

Wisdom, like water in a well, takes a bucket of patience to draw it up.

Knowledge lies in the brain, but wisdom in the heart.

Choose wisely, separating wants from needs.

Important is silence and aloneness.
In the quiet of being alone, the heart speaks.

Guilt and grudges are heavy loads, which can crush health and joy.

If you think me better than I am,
I will put forth effort to show you the better side.

A word of praise can lift a man's shoulders, and he will stride tall.
His heart responds, "Yes, that is me."

Christian growth is best achieved by simple belief
in the goodness of the person.

Rain

Rain.
Wet drops falling.
Splat.
And once again came the rains.
While on the leaves
The dry dust streaked.
Absorbed.
And then run in muddy flow
Back to the good earth.

Reapers

Oh reapers, awake, do not tarry,
For the harvest now is ready.
Fast time is moving, rushing on.
Comes the morning; breaks the dawn.
Reapers, gather from the field:
The bounty crop the seed did yield.
Let harvest work be finished—done—
Ere the setting of the sun.
Working, working all together.
Working, working, fainting not.
Fruit on branches, hanging down,
Be it gathered ere it fall upon the ground.
Time waits not upon the will of man.
Harvest now while yet you can.
Gather in, nor count the cost.
'Tis not God's will that one be lost.
Then with the harvest, we'll ascend on high.
To meet our Lord there in the sky.

Rebirth

Sweet, dainty blossom
On the tree of life,
Filled with a fragrance all your own.
Falling swiftly to the ground,
'Neath life's buffeting storm.
Yet life's not gone,
For nestled in the heart of love,
Fresh fruit is born.

Rending Sorrow

The Maker called, and you hurried on to answer,
        leaving us behind, who loved you so.
An ache, a loneliness, an empty dream we
        hold, though we have sorrow in our heart in
        our
        lives it can't be so.
Your work here was completed: ours has just
        begun.
We must go on living, filling each
        tomorrow, maybe we can join you when our
        work
        is done.
Though I long to join you there, I must stay
        and raise our son.

Oh, heart, be quiet. Still thy murmur: Stop your palpitation.
The life you lived is past,
Sorrow that rends asunder.
Let it go.

Revolving Earth

The earth upon its axis turns,
Marked by rise and set of sun.
Yet racing on in orbit flung,
Round and round it makes its run.
And we, who upon this chariot ride,
Though well aware of night and tide,
Feel not the ever, onward flow,
As through the universe we silent go.

Shepherds Haste

Away across the ocean,
Near a little town,
Shepherds tending sheep,
Had bedded them all down.

To Bethlehem, not far away,
Weary travelers made their way.
The inns were filled to overflow;
There was no place for folks to go.

Joseph begged, "My wife needs rest.
Even a stall would be most blessed."
And so it was in fresh new hay,
Christ, the newborn babe did lay.

'Twas then that angels, glowing bright,
With their chorus filled the night,
And frightened shepherds heard them say,
"To Bethlehem, haste, haste away."

And haste they did. Left all behind,
To bow in awe before their find.
A tiny babe sent from above,
Lulled to sleep by a turtledove.

What a wondrous gift sent from on high,
To remind us all that God is nigh.
So lift your voice in carols gay.
Rejoice! Rejoice! 'Tis Christmas day.

Short Verses by Pearl

Holy, holy, holy is my God.
Straight the path He set for me,
Though the path I cannot see.
He is there to guide;
We'll walk together side-by-side,
If His word, I will obey,
And on the path I will to stay.
For He's my God.

Can God clean a sinful heart?
Yes, He can.
Can God make it good as new?
Yes, He can.
Does sin so great abound?
Yes, it does.

Reincarnate King,
Love reaching out to enfold the unlovely
Scarred and marred am I.
Hold me.
Enfold me.

Don't let life get you down.
There's much ahead to treasure,
But seek for it with all your might.
Rejoice in every pleasure.

God's commands are my delight.
They were written down in stone.
But within my heart, better still,
The desire to do His blessed will.
For He is my God,
And I love Him so.
God cares for me.
          I am safe under His wing.
        Come on under.

On mountaintop did leap the hart,
So nimble were his feet,
But now me think the time to calmer walk,
And let the younger, heights to seek.

All honor,
All glory,
All peace,
All joy,
All things good,
Come from the Lord.

Silently, the Flocks of Sheep

Silently, the flocks of sheep,
Huddled close, were fast asleep.
While the shepherds, seated near,
Kept watchful eye for lion or bear.

But what is this dispels the night?
Awesome glory brings such fright.
The shepherds dozing, fast awake.
The calm now shattered, how they quake,

As angels coming from on high,
Around the shepherds, fill the sky.
Peace! Peace! In joy, the angels sing.
From hill and vale, the echoes ring.

Haste! Oh, haste! Be on your way.
Behold the wonder of this day.
To Bethlehem, how fast they sped,
Seeking a babe in a manger bed.

In awe they stand before their find,
The Savior, King of all mankind.
So now do we, on Christmas Eve,
The beauty and wonder also perceive.

In awe, let us sing forth His praise.
In awe, let us His anthems raise,
To worship our King the same as they,
And have a merry Christmas Day.

Simon of Cyrene, to his beloved sons, Alexander and Rufus

(Based on Luke 23:26–47)

Strange and wonderful things have happened on my trip. I can scarce restrain myself until I return to tell you face-to-face. For wonders of wonders, I have seen the Messiah, the Son of God, and more than that, I have touched him. Such rapture and glory fills my soul, but I must tell you first of my entering into that great city, Jerusalem. As I entered the city, it was very early on the preparation day and an especially important preparation day it was. Jew's had come from the most distant places for the Passover feast. They were packed into the city and spread out onto every available spot. There were people, people, people, some rolling up their bedding, others preparing the morning meal over campfires, smoke and cooking smells filled the air. Such a clamoring—shouting and singing and children everywhere, running, playing and having wonderful fun. Everyone was filled with the holiday spirit. Surely nothing could mar such sheer joy of being alive and among friends, some of which had not greeted each other since the last Passover feast.

Suddenly! It was the strangest feeling: a fear seemed to fill every heart. Children left their playmates and scurried to their mothers. On every side could be heard whisperings and wondering of what had caused this strange uneasiness.

In that still, deadly calm I could hear a heavy rumbling and made my way through the streets toward the sound. What a sight met my eyes! On the outer rim of a great mob were people weeping, some loud and openly, some moaning quietly in great distress, some tightlipped and stony-eyed. Passing through this rim of weeping humanity, I came upon such a mixture of people, the very dregs of the slums, pushing, screaming and cursing, mingled with the temple priests, teachers of the law and the Roman soldiers trying to maintain order. Truly, I have written it. What a shock to see the servants of the most high God conducting themselves in such a manner, and they seemed to be the source that was fueling the discord of the mob.

What great sin has been committed? I wondered in my heart. For by now, I could see that there were three prisoners, each struggling under a crucifix. One was dropping further and further behind the other two. As I approached closer, I could see and feel that this man was the cause of the deep feelings displayed there.

The soldiers in charge of the prisoners were brutal, vile men, prodding the crowd to make way and laughing coarsely among themselves as they lashed out at their prisoners. The one prisoner never once raised his head nor uttered a sound, so unlike the other two, who were cursing their captors, and spitting and jeering back at the crowd that surrounded them.

As I looked I saw this quiet, submissive man stumble under the heavy cross. The soldier nearest him raised a whip bringing it down violently across a back—already raw and open from previous beatings. Once more the whip was raised, and with such cursing and shouting for the poor man to move on, the soldier brought the whip down across his head, and I saw a crown of thorns dig their barbs deep into his brow.

Such anger at the inhumanity of man and such sympathy for the weak, staggering man welled up in me when he fell with the weight of the cross crushing him to the dusty road. All else faded from my mind as I pushed through the crowd, taking upon my own back the blow that was once more aimed at that pathetic figure. Such compassion I have never felt. I lifted that heavy cross to my own shoulder and held it there while I reached with the other hand to help the weak, struggling man to his feet once more.

As I touched him, those dark, pain-filled eyes turned upon me: such glory filled my soul. I felt like kneeling—I was in the presence of God himself—and would surely have done so but was brought back to an awareness of the circumstances by the loud laughter of the soldiers, who mockingly said. "You would carry a cross? It's yours to bear." My heart leaped for joy. They could not know how gladly I carried that symbol of sin. Tacked to the cross were the words "King of the Jews."

As I bore the cross beside that staggering figure, I finally was able to mutter, "It is true. You are the Messiah!" Once more those sad, pain-filled eyes turned on me, and for a fleeting moment, a look of joy leaped into their dark depths.

I have much to tell you of the happenings of that sad, dark day—for dark it truly was there on the hill, Golgotha. He was stripped of his robe, which the guards immediately cast lots for. Soon to be nail-pierced hands were held fast to that crude cross by the soldiers. The heavy blows pounded at the nails, and the crucifix was roughly thrust upright in a prepared hole. Gasping for each breath, he hung exposed before the unruly mob. He cried with a loud, pain filled cry, "Father, forgive them for they know not what they do."

Who was he asking God to forgive? The merciless soldiers who drove the nails? The mocking, jeering crowd? The now penitent thief who cried out "We are sinners deserving death. He is innocent! Remember me when you come into your kingdom." Had he not been brought to the slaughter, even as the innocent Passover lamb was slain for the sins of others?

My own sins overwhelmed me. My heart cried out "Lord, forgive me, too." As those sad eyes met mine for a fleeting moment, I felt at peace.

His cry for sinners started a tirade from the priests. "If you be the Messiah, come down from the cross and we will believe you."

This taunt was taken up by the mob as they jeered, "Others he could save; himself he cannot."

He cried with a loud, anguished voice, "My Father, my Father, why have you forsaken me? As if in answer to his cry, the sun stopped shining and a deep, eerie darkness covered all the heavens from the sixth to the ninth hour. The great sea of people, who up to this time had been taunting and jeering, suddenly fell silent and began slinking away into the darkness. The priests, too, now seemed filled with a strange foreboding and most hurried away into that terrible darkness. Soon all that were left were the centurion and his men, a few of the priests and teachers of the law, and but a small remnant of the crowd.

A few weeping men and women now drew nearer to the cross. At the ninth hour, Jesus cried out again, "Father, into Thy hands I commit my spirit." When he had said this, he died. The centurion saw that he was dead and praised God saying, "Surely this was a righteous man." At the demands of the priests and teachers of the law, a spear pierced his side. The remaining people gathered to see for themselves what had taken place. Then beating their breasts, they slunk away. Then I, too, left the scene. The sacred Passover Sabbath, which had started out with such joy, was a subdued day indeed. There are many things to tell of those days after the crucifixion, but I will save them to tell you when I arrive home.

Sisters

Sisters are like the sunshine.
Bound by ties, they always stay,
Held close within our memories,
Even when the dark clouds hide
The sunbeams all away.
How our hearts do welcome
The bright and warming rays,
Of sister's love wrapped round us,
On the cold and bitter days.
And as the years pass by us,
Leaving joints and bones that creak,
How welcome is the warm sun,
Putting roses on our cheek.
Without our sisters by our side,
How dull and dreary be the path,
That reaching through the distance,
Brings us home at last:
I'm glad God gave me sisters.
Jewels each, most precious treasure.
The warmth you shed in my life,
Can ne'er be held in cup nor measure.

Sleep Little Ones

(Written in memory of cousin Louis' grandchildren, killed in a home fire)

Steep, my little ones.
Sleep, my precious gems.
This old world can never reach
To hurt my loves again.
Held warm and safe you'll always be,
Enfolded in the arms of Him
Who loves you more than life or death.
And when my time has come,
I'll join you there,
And watch in pure delight,
As angels waft you to my arms
In the land where there's no more night.
In joy then we'll weep,
And remember no more the pain.
Oh! Babies mine, I scarce can wait
To hold you in my arms again.
So sleep, my little ones,
Sleep, my precious gems,
Until united we shall stand,
On the golden streets with Jesus.

Snow Mobile

(New Year's Day when the boys were teens)

Bill called from work to give me a phone number of a man who rented snowmobiles, saying if I would go get one, we would go on the snow the next day, New Year's Day. That sounded like fun so as soon as I hung up, I called the number. The man said he was going to be over south of town, and if I would meet him there, he would have the snowmobile with him. I told him I had a station wagon, and he said the snowmobile would fit right in the back of it. When I got to the address be gave me, he was busy and said he would be right with me. So, I waited until he was free. Then he backed his pickup up to the station wagon and slid the snowmobile into the back of it—that is until he got to the handlebars. They were several inches too high and just wouldn't fit.

He said he had a trailer over north of town. If I would drive over there, he would close up the shop where we were and meet me there. I found the address he gave me and waited for him and waited and waited. Finally, he arrived and said that he didn't have the keys to the shop where we were and that he would have to go home and get them—that he didn't live too far away and would be back soon. Winter nights are short, and it began to get dark. Still he wasn't back.

When he returned, he had a trailer with two snowmobiles on it and suggested we drive up the street to a service station so there would be lights. Then he would transfer one snowmobile to his pickup and hook up the trailer for me. We drove to the station and he started to unload the snowmobile onto his pickup when he said he was tired and really didn't want to unload it. If I would take both, he would give me the second one real cheap. This sounded good to me as I was more than ready to get home.

It had taken all afternoon, but the boys were delighted when I arrived home with two snowmobiles. Beautiful, sunshiny New Year's Day, we loaded the car with gloves, coats, snowshoes, hot chocolate, and a thermos of hot chili beans. We drove miles and miles and miles up the mountains until we arrived at a spot where there was a little aide road that wound around and round under the big trees and back into the forest. Of course that little road was all snowed in because the snowplow only cleared the big roads. It was a perfect place to ride the snowmobiles.

The boys could hardly wait as we unloaded the snowmobiles. They unfastened and pushed the first snowmobile off the trailer, climbed on, pushed the starter, and the snowmobile was ready to go. How impatient they were to get the second one unloaded. Finally, it was ready to go, and the starter pushed, but nothing happened. The starter was pushed again and again, but it just wouldn't start. Daddy checked the gas. It was okay. He checked the battery. The lights came on; the starter growled; the battery was okay. He checked all the wires and connections. they were okay. But the snowmobile wouldn't start.

We spent the morning taking turns riding: two at a time as that was how many the snowmobile would carry. While two were riding the other two were building a snow rabbit. (We never built anything as mundane as snowman.) Around noon, we had our hot chili beans and chocolate. Then Strider took off alone on the snowmobile. Strider was gone quite a while. When he returned, Phalin went off alone following Strider's trail to see where Strider had gone. In the meantime, we still would push that starter to see if the second snowmobile might start. While Phalin was gone, another car pulled off the freeway where we were. When the man was told about the snowmobile that wouldn't start, he looked at it and told us we would never get it started as there was a hole in the fuel line. So we pushed it beck upon the trailer and fastened it down. When Phalin returned, we would head for home. We waited and waited. He should have been back long ago. I told Daddy and Strider I was going to start walking back on the trail because I could imagine him having run in a tree or over the bluff. Something was wrong or he would have been back. So I started walking. It's very hard to walk in soft snow. After I started, Daddy caught up with me and said he would go with me. I told him that was not a good idea as the snowmobile would only carry two people out again. If he was going, I would go back to the car. Now with Daddy walking in the soft snow, I had two people to worry about.

It was starting to get late, and snow clouds came over making it darker. I couldn't think of a single station or even a house where I could get help for miles and miles. We needed a big light for sure and a snowmobile to get over the snow, and right there on the trailer were both. I said to Strider, "We are going to unfasten that snowmobile and push it off the trailer. Then we are going to ask God to start it. Then you are going to drive in and see what's wrong." So we pushed it off the trailer and knelt there in the snow and asked God to start it. Strider climbed on, pushed the starter, and it started right up. Away he went.

It wasn't long before we are all headed safely home again. I often marvel how God was answering my prayer before I prayed by giving me that second snowmobile the day before I needed it. Isn't He a marvelous God? (Isaiah 65:24, "Before they call I will answer.")

Song of the Seraphim

1.
Praise ye the Father;
Amen! Amen!
Praise ye the Father;
Hallelujah, Amen!

2.
Praise ye dear Jesus;
Amen! Amen!
Praise ye dear Jesus;
Hallelujah, Amen!

3
Praise the Holy Spirit;
Amen! Amen!
Praise the Holy Spirit;
Hallelujah, Amen!

(chorus)
Hallelujah! Hallelujah!
Hallelujah, Amen!
Hallelujah! Hallelujah!
Praise Him again.

Sowing Seed

God has sent his children out
With good seed to scatter all about.
If off to town you have to go,
Scatter seed that it may grow.
And if dear children, you're off to school,
Plant your seed by the golden rule.

In hearts of family, friend, and peer,
The fertile ground of those most dear.
Plant your seed and watch it grow,
It's the nearest place for you to sow.
God will water, and God will weed.
Your only job is plant the seed.

Spring

A new year has started on its way.
Fast the months do fly.
Longer and longer grows the day,
And birds are in the sky.

The fly begins to buzz again.
The skeeter starts to bite.
The sky begins to look like rain,
And crickets chirp all night.

The garden starts to sprout and grow.
Lovers start to sing.
Children want outside to play.
These are the signs of spring.

Step by Step

Step by step, step by step, in step for Jesus.
Soon the work is done.
Step by step, step by step, for Jesus
Can be such fun.
Be not a' sitting; be up and on your way,
And while you are a' stepping,
Don't forget to pray.

Step by step, step by step, in step for Jesus.
Thank Him for your two feet
To carry you about.
Thank Him for your two lips
that can sing and shout.
Step by step, step by step, in step for Jesus.
Through your lungs fresh air does flow.
Get off your chair—away you go.

Take Me Home

Precious Lord, take me home:
Of this world I've weary grown.
Take me home to pastures green,
Where sin and greed are never seen.
Take me home to be with Thee;
Precious Lord, I weary be.

Tell Me Shepherds

Tell me, shepherds, once again,
Tell the story from start to end.
Tell about that night of old,
When the angels, you did behold.

Tell how you were filled with fright,
As their glory filled the night.
How "Peace on earth" the angels sang,
How the hills and valleys rang.

Tell the message they did bring,
"In a manger, go find your King."
Tell how, in haste, you left the sheep,
Hurried to Bethlehem where all did sleep.

Tell how you spread the message round,
As you searched the streets of town,
That in a manger full of hay,
Christ the Savior lay that day.

How is it they did not know?
How is it they missed the glow?
Tell us shepherds, tell it bold,
That we the Christ Child may behold.

The Bible

The Bible, Thy Holy Word,
A path to righteousness does lay,
A light to shine on the perfect way.
But where Thy Word? Time hurries on:
No time to seek, no time to read,
No time to plant the living seed.
Thy law must be within our heart,
Not in a book somewhere apart.
In our mind must be its root,
Not covered there by rust or soot.
The choice is ours and ours alone,
The things we place upon Thy throne.
Our mind the altar, sanctified by Thy grace,
Protected from the lure of human race.
Holy Spirit sheltered there.
We Praise Thy Holy Name:
That it be glorified
Not ours.

The Butterfly

A butterfly, with silken wings outspread,
In my garden came to dine,
Gliding softly, settled down
On the blossom of the honeysuckle vine.
And as she sipped the nectar there,
I watched in pure delight,
As the wonder of creation
Was opened to my sight.

The Garden Temptation

The constellation, Orion, stretched across the sky in all its splendor, and Lucifer cast but one longing look, allowed himself but one fleeting memory. Then he raised his rich voice in song that vibrated up and down the lovely valleys and hills, echoing and resounding, for never voice so rich and deep—no bell, nor harp, nor horn could ring with truer, deeper tone. Beauty was not only in the tone, but this lovely creature beamed and glowed; the sapphire and onyx, Yea! all the precious stones of his apparel scarce could hold its glow against this majestic cherubim. And his song—a song of victory:

> "I, the covering cherub,
> Wise above all created being,
> Stood long beside the throne of God,
> Served in deep adoration,
> The Creator of the universe.
> Being daily at His side,
> Increased in wisdom,
> Until I, the greatest of creation,
> Was changed likewise into a God.
> This planet earth, my first domain.
> Oh, yes! Faithful host who follow me,
> Angels need no fencing law.
> Freedom now to you I bring.
> Bow down before me, your new king."

And from every hill and vale resounded angel choir, "Hail, Lucifer, the morning star." No response from out the garden heard, but won't be long 'til they emerge.

On the far side of this new world, animals stood a moment, lifting heads as if to catch a far-off sound, then continued their play, romping in the evening glow, staying close to man and woman there in the garden. Once again raised eyes to Orion, that great constellation. A flash of brilliance they had caught in the corridor of the heaven leading to the celestial city.

Lord of the world brought forth by His Word, in the cool of the evening, came to be with His new creation there in the garden: A Father with His loved ones inquiring of their guardian angel, "What say they today? What spoke they? Did they ask of Me? Do they love the gifts I have given?" Anxiously inquiring of their safety and obedience there in the garden. And ere He left his loved ones to the care of angel guardians, bid He once again, "Go not near the tree of knowledge." So sheltered like new babes, made in image of their God, clothed in glory, left He them there in the garden.

How great if they but had the knowledge which lies within their reach. Babes! Ha! gods they are and gods shall be. I must help them to the tree of knowledge. And daily came he, Lucifer, to view from afar, the garden, its inhabitants, and that tree.

In the branches of that tree rested a serpent, with his wing scales glittering translucent colors like jewels in the sunlight. His splendor caught the eyes of Eve who had wandered for a moment from the side of her beloved, there in the garden wandered near the tree, forbidden. Closer still she drew in sheer delight to view the beauty of this creature in the tree, scarce aware it was the tree of knowledge. In cunning guise and lying wonder, enticed she was to eat the fruit thereof, and Adam joined in her transgression. Oh! That the day be forever stricken from the record. That it might be erased forever more.

Naked, bereft of all their glory, sewed they garments of fig leaves, hiding from their Maker—

hiding from the Lord who loved them. Animals, sensing something missing, fled before their presence.

The Lord, their Creator, the Beloved, called them into His presence. Tears in eyes, sob in voice,

sent He them from the garden: For cursed is the land where sin abides and cursed must not be the garden.

Cherubim guarded with flaming sword ever-turning, guarding well the tree of life, guarding at the entrance to the garden. For death is master where sin abides, and eternal life forbidden. He who breaks the law of God can enter not into His garden.

Don't be drawn to everything that glitters. It may be Satan in disguise.

The Lord Is Coming

The Lord is coming: He hears our cry,
Coming with angels through the heaving sky,
Coming for those He claims His own,
Coming to take His children home.
No more tears; no more sorrows,
Endless ages of tomorrows.

The Lord's Message

There is a message, long been given,
By God's Holy Spirit, brought from Heaven,
A message of woe to an unregenerate heart,
A message of hope if you take the Lord's part.
The judgment has begun. The books opened wide.
Christ, the Mediator, is He on your side?

He is just and merciful.
He is quick to forgive,
For He was tempted and tried;
Knows our weakness and pride.
Over our sins He has cried.
Never once did He chide.

The Ark of the Testament sits there, too.
The commandments within it were given to you.
Did you keep them, my children, count them, all ten?
When you faltered and failed, did you try once again?
The angels recorded from the day of your birth,
Each thought and each action you did here on earth.

Nothing is hid from the all-seeing eye,
But all can be saved, that's why Christ came to die.
He can erase all the pages filled up with your sin.
Ask Him and "forgiven" will be written there-in.
Then in glory ascending, you'll meet Him on high.
When with angels descending, He comes in the sky.

The Mirror

The face in the mirror, is it really me?
It's not the face I used to see,
And yet familiar in some small way.
As I look, I scarce can turn away.

Oh, thou who does intently stare,
In the remnant of the past I see,
What once was, is it still there?
Or forever gone, no more to be.
I have not seen before.
Wiser, weaker, sadder, I cannot tell,
But gone the face I knew so well.

By searching could I find the one,
That face I used to know?
I think not for time but marches on,
And when 'tis past 'tis gone.
Memory too fades fast away,
And then it's unclear face gives sway
To the face that now I see,
The one that now stares back at me.

Whence and when did wrinkles first appear?
And thinning hair? And sagging skin?
When I from the mirror flee,
No more wrinkles do I see.
Don't know that old gal,
Familiar though she seem.
Could be I'll soon awake
And find 'twas all a dream.

The only thing that holds as true,
The mirror shows no longer young are you.
Those years are gone so hold the tears.
Faces change with passing years.
And this morning, as I stopped to stare,
It was a strange face lurching there.
I looked awhile and walked away,
In the mirror it must stay.

The Tree

The tree with fruit, full hung.
A glittering serpent sat there in the boughs,
Nibbling, nibbling, a bite from here, a bite from there.
"Come eat with me, beauteous Queen."
He rolled his eyes and fanned his wings.
He sighed once and again he sighed.
No Adam stood there at her side.
"'Tis wondrous fruit I've found from off this tree—
Such joy, such pure delight.
It fair does make my belly dance."
Saying thus he took another bite.
"Come fair lady, be my guest.
Join me in this wondrous quest.
For knowledge is dispensed here.
Come fair lady, have no fear."
All the while his eyes were cast
On mother Eve, beneath its boughs.
Wondering eyes beheld each bite.
And stirred not herself to leave the site.
Serpent glided to a lower bough,
Plucked again from off the tree.
Bid mother Eve to taste and see.
Thinking in her heart, I'll just look.
Reaching forth with trembling hand she took.
Then came Adam looking for his mate;
Saw in her hand the fruit she ate.
His form in fear and anguish shook.
As from her hand a bite he took.
"What shall we do? What shall we do?
What e'er your fate, I'll share it too."
Tears of agony ran down their faces.
He held her close in sweet embraces.
As glory dimmed and disappeared.
Naked wept they in the garden.

Thou Creator

Thou Creator, great and wise,
High above the starry skies,
Always near, loving, and fair;
Never holding back Your care.
Kind to all, both friend and foe,
Sending rain, sunshine or snow.
Giver of life, hear me now,
As I, in adoration, to Thee bow.
Visit me this very hour.
In wisdom fill me with Thy power.
No glory mine, but all Thine own,
Great and Mighty, Holy One.

Thy Word

A path to righteousness does lay:
A light to shine on the perfect way.
But where Thy Word? Time hurries on.
No time to seek, no time to read,
No time to plant the living seed.
Thy law must be within our heart,
Not in a book somewhere apart.
In our mind must be its root:
Not covered there by rust or soot.
The choice is ours and ours alone,
The things we place upon Thy throne.
Our mind the altar, sanctified by Thy grace,
Protected from the lure of human race.
Holy Spirit sheltered there,
We praise Thy Holy Name:
That it be glorified
By our every thought and deed.

Thy Word A Light

Thy Word, oh, Lord, is light.
Thy Word is life and power.
This word of mine,
Which I use with so little thought,
Can weld a sword so sharp.
As to rend a soul.
Or with healing, meld.
My word can change a thought,
Can brighten up a day,
Can bring sorrow, tears, or joy.
Oh, tongue, be careful what you say.

Time of Growing

There is a time of growing,
A time of shaping, a time of molding.
As on this earth we spend our years,
God gives us joy as well as tears.
Some times the furnace, stoked is high,
The dross in passing makes us cry;
But he who holds us to the fire,
Ever watching is His eye.

'Tis Christmas

Tales of flying deer and Santa's sleigh,
And Rudolph's nose to light the way.
Christmas carols fill the air.
Shoppers hurry, scurry everywhere.
The tree is decked in tinsel bright,
And counters laden, what a sight!
The table's set with the best plates,
And presents 'neath the tree awaits.
Pause awhile and find a way,
To thank the Lord on His birthday.

'Tis Gone

How can life so quickly go?
No more than forest fire be quenched,
As though the very fuel of life be stayed.
How can it be? And yet 'tis so.
A crumpled flower cannot grow.

Trusting God

Jesus knows—
The heartache,
The rejection,
The anger,
That you feel.
That frustration
Feeds and feeds
Rebellion.
This do not allow.

Choices are often made
Because of convenience
Rather than a careful
Thought,

How easy it would be to
Confess our sins and ask
Forgiveness if we could pile
On all the excuses we could*
Think of.
(These would seem to make
us the victim instead of the
perpetrator)

Snap decisions,
Unforgotten bits and pieces,
Clutter that cling,
That appear and disappear
As quickly as they came,
But always there
Like some wrinkle in time
And space, It won't erase.
No logic, no excuse can
Sugarcoat or hide.
It chips away at our ego
And feeds upon our pride.
So, battered, torn at life's
Decisions do we mourn,

And wish them all away,
But they just stay

We stand in the place of
God as a visible example to
Family, neighbors, friends
And all we meet, showing
His character. by planting
Thus His seed.

The Old Testament reveals
God's character, His
Reaching out to save people;
His council through His
Prophets and His sons.
The New Testament is a last
Final call, a message of His great love.

Dry bones, flesh and spirit—
Gone.
God opens graves, brings
Them up, and takes them home.

May our life show our love,
Patience, and compassion.
May our ego be put under,
And our life reflect the God
We love. May every shadow
Of our evil life be cleaned
Away that our reflection be
True to His dear grace.

My God is whole, complete,
A gracious Father, Provider,
Discipliner, Encourager,
A solid foundation.

Advance unless God says,
"Stop where you are." You
Have already been led
Safely this far.

Men in the Valley of Humility
Depend on God.
Upon reaching the pinnacle,
They remember not their need
Of God.

Be the leader of the family
God has given.
Maybe is not God's will.
Go forward on your knees.
The battle is the Lord's.
He will fight our battles,
Faith is our victory.

Clouds will fill the sky.
Loud the sound of trumpets
Cry, as earth splits wide and
The call is given, "Awake ye
Dead; arise and live." While
Angels waft them to meet
Family and Jesus in the air,
Will you be there my son?
My daughter; will you be
There? Long we waited for
The victory of this day. Hang
On. Hang on.

Weep not nor fret,
Trust your God.
Believe His word.
There is no war but He
Allows.

Tomorrow we wilt be okay
Because God is in control,
Today and always in
Control; disciplining,
Teaching, holding in check,
A strong foundation,
Allowing what will lead us to
Salvation.

To Be or Not To Be

To be or not to be. To opt or not to opt. To choose this or that. So many choices that are ours, and each can have a great impact on our future, shaping our lives for good or for evil. Some, like the choices of Eve and Adam, also influence those touched by our lives for generations to come. Rarely are we the lone recipient of our choices. Few are they that we remember with peace and contentment. Many are remembered with remorse and even shame. God can forgive, has even paid the penalty for our transgressions, but He cannot erase the event. It is written in the annals of history, never to be undone. We cannot go back. The ripples reach so far from the source as to seem to be a source unto themselves. They may have set the future for as long as earth exists. Think long on that idle word or act. What influence might it have on the actions of another?

Trust

Last night my soul was troubled.
It seethed, and jumped, and spun.
I knelt beside my bed and prayed,
And relaxation come.
Somehow the trouble vanished.
Unaware of the going was I.
I slept and the problem was solved.
No longer needed I cry.
Though I am unaware of the answer,
I know that it will be right
For God in His mercy and kindness
Has listened and solved my plight.

Two Sons in The Vineyard

There was a husbandman who called his two Sons to him one morning and said, "The crops are ripe, ready for harvest. I want you to go out today and gather the fruit into the barns that there may be food until the time of harvest returns to the land in another year."

The older son looked upon his father. There was a smile on his face and a twinkle in his eyes. Then he spoke, "Be cheerful, father. I will go and bring in an abundant crop."

The observer would have thought, *Would that I had a son such as he. What joy to my old age would be such a son.*

But the father's heart was troubled as he looked on his beloved son. He knew the inner workings of his heart, and the father watched with sadness as the son departed from his presence.

Gathering bow and arrow, food, and bedroll, the older son departed for the high country to enjoy himself in the forest for a season, never returning until the crops were gathered and stored.

"I was going to do it when I returned," he said.

The younger son on hearing the request of his father, fumed within himself. Had he not planned a pleasant day? There were places to go and things to see that did not include reaping in the field.

"No. I will not go today." The young man, scowling and frowning, turned to his father and said, "I won't do it. I won't. I have other things to do. I can't be bothered."

One who looked on would have thought, *I am glad I do not have a son such he. What a trial he would be in my old age.*

But the father of this beloved son, whom he had watched over year after year, only smiled and his heart was light within him. He was at peace for he knew the inner workings of the heart of his boy. The young son, leaving his father's presence, went into the field and worked without ceasing until all the crops were gathered and stored in the barns.

Under His Wing

(Based on Psalms 91)

In the shadow of His wings,
A place where joy and peace abideth,
In the shadow of His wing,
From the terror of the night He'll hide us.
In the shadow of His wings,
Hearts of peace, without the fears.
In the shadow of His wings,
Our trust in him, no more tears.

He'll soothe away our sorrow,
We need not fear tomorrow,
Need not fear the darkest night,
Nor arrows that at noon do strike.
Though a thousand fall on every hand,
We are circled by an angel band.
He will quickly answer when we call.
He will hold us up that we not fall.

Ever near Him we must stay,
Nor seek to leave the narrow way.
He is faithful: His Word is true.
His promise is, "I'm coming back for you."

Vanity

A gentle breeze whisked tendrils out of place.
Before the mirror, that very morn, long he spent,
Placing each just so, now careless blown.
Such vanity to cause distress? Not so!
With the bright day and gentle breeze,
Vanity, too, has blown away.
A freer mood and crown of hair loose tossed,
Long gone the somber soul,
And in its place a step more gay.
And you, oh, gentle breeze, blow on.

Wandering With a Dream

On grassy knolls beat down with snow,
And hills made bright with rain,
I walked alone not caring where,
Nor from whence I came.

Hope was shining bright before me.
Onward went my trail.
I saw not the mud beneath my feet,
Nor felt that I would fall.

I had my thoughts to help and guide me.
Gloom did not know the way.
With laughter in my eyes and song upon my lip,
I spent a happy day.

I had my thoughts to guide me
To lead me all the way.
Happy looks and happy song
Were with me all the day.

Weep Tears of Joy

Weep tears of joy, but not despair.
We'll see our loved ones over there,
in God's kingdom bright and fair.

We were given life for a short space.
What joy will shine from Jesus' face,
When loved ones are united by His grace.

The seed that grew in this world of strife,
In heaven again will spring to life,
And fairer be and sweeter still.

When Gone This Day

When gone this day
      the daily sun,
So is the work you
      might have done.
You pass but once
      along this way,
So what must be done,
      do it today.

When I'm Gone

This old abode has had its day.
It's served its owner well.
No longer safe the hallowed halls:
The windows darkened stay.
No laughter from an open door,
No tears from sorrow flow,
And if some joy or comfort be,
Remembered for a while,
It too will pass with passing time,
Like embers from fire.
So loved ones carry on.
Don't stand long in sorrow,
Nor mourn to long the loss.
There's only rest where I have gone:
And time is measured not.
And if, per chance, the Lord desires,
To look again upon my face,
I'll rise at trumpet call to see you there,
But only by His grace.

When Life Is Gone

Sharp the wounds inflicted
When the enemy of life rends yet another soul,
And life is gone.
Call loudly, "Awake! Arise!"
None heeds the call,
For life in passing heeds no call
But passes on.
Nor forgotten shall you be,
For in recesses of the heart
Will linger memories of thee.
And even more enduring,
In the book of life insuring,
To be read upon the Lord's returning,
"You are Mine."
Can that which God holds fast
Slip so easily from His grasp?
Nay! Not so! Sleep on.
A little longer rest 'til the trumpet blast.
Then wake where now you're sleeping.
With loving eyes, you'll greet Him;
With gladness greet the dawn.
How warm the embraces
As we see each other's faces,
Fathers, mothers, sisters, brothers,
On that longed for resurrection day.

Where Can I Find Thee?

Holy Father, great and mighty I AM,
Where can I find Thee? And yet where are You not found?
In all directions of the sky I seek Thee.
Signs of Your presence are in every star and cloud.
On the surface of the earth I seek Thee.
In crevices and rock, in tree and grassy plain,
Vast desert and streams show the beauty You maintain.
Eyes behold your glory spread in bits and pieces here and there.
Like some giant puzzle scattered through earth and sea and air.

Why Me, Lord?

Why me, Lord?
This is not the way I choose to go.
This path I do not care to walk.
The way is long.
Familiar things are gone.
And fear of the unknown
Makes me want to turn and flee.
Why me, Lord?
I do not want to walk this way.

If I would walk with Thee,
Then I must follow where you go,
Though strange and unfamiliar things,
Loom on every side.
I'm free to return from whence I came.
But I would walk with Thee.
My life, my love, my friend,
With Thee, I would abide.

With Tearful Eyes

With tearful eyes we watched
Her suffer and saw her fade away.
Although we could not bear to lose her,
We could not bid her stay.

God saw that she was getting tired,
And a cure was not to be.
So He put His arms around her
And whispered, "Come with Me."

Wonders of Spring

The wonders of spring in my garden sing:
Hummingbird, robin, and dragonfly,
Bumblebee, ladybug, and butterfly.
In their beauty, flit on gossamer wing,
While the roses, dandelion, geranium, too,
Iris blossoms: red, white, yellow, and blue.
Fruit trees in blossom, the things I adore,
I find all them just outside of my door.
How wise our God; How loving is He;
He placed all these wonders right
Where I can see.

You Watch Over Me

You watch over me, and I am unaware.
Through trials and joys, You are there.
Faithful, Your love has fenced me in—
Shown me the ugliness of sin.
A place You have prepared for me.
A place that I so long to see.
A place within your Holy Realm,
Such joys there will thus o'erwhelm.
You will return and take me there,
And gone this chasm of despair.

TEACH Services, Inc.
P U B L I S H I N G

We invite you to view the complete
selection of titles we publish at:
www.TEACHServices.com

We encourage you to write us
with your thoughts about this,
or any other book we publish at:
info@TEACHServices.com

TEACH Services' titles may be purchased in
bulk quantities for educational, fund-raising,
business, or promotional use.
bulksales@TEACHServices.com

Finally, if you are interested in seeing
your own book in print, please contact us at:
publishing@TEACHServices.com
We are happy to review your manuscript at no charge.

www.ingramcontent.com/pod-product-compliance
Lightning Source LLC
Chambersburg PA
CBHW071216160426
43196CB00012B/2321